Gari Jones: Three Plays

Wretch
Somewhere Else
Toilet

Published by Playdead Press 2013

A CIP catalogue record for this book is available from the British Library.

ISBN 978-0-9576792-2-1

Printed by BPUK

Playdead Press
www.playdeadpress.com

Gari Jones is an established and experienced Director and Writer. With over twenty years experience, his work has been seen at the Royal National Theatre, the Almeida, the Old Vic, the Young Vic, in the West End, on Broadway, in squat venues, churches, car-parks, night clubs, warehouses and has also toured extensively throughout the UK and internationally, as well as in many other Theatres and Drama Schools. He has devised, worked with writers on new plays, directed contemporary and classical work, and created a range of site-specific, multi-media & cross-art work.

Front Cover Image 'Skull Rose' by Benson Koo
www.facebook.com/bensonkooart

This book is dedicated to my amazing wife and children, without whom I would have lost all hope.

Wretch
11

Somewhere Else
51

Toilet
111

Wretch (Fragments) Part Two

First performed at the Mercury Theatre, Colchester, June 2011.

Directed and performed by Gari Jones

Designer – Amy Yardley
Animator – Vanja Sheremetkoski
Lighting Designer – Emily Holmden
Tour Lighting Designer – Ben Payne
Sound Designer – Chris Murray
Stage Manager/Make-Up Designer – Deborah Stubbington

Wretch subsequently played further runs at the Mercury Theatre, Colchester Arts Centre, the Edinburgh Festival and toured Internationally.

With thanks to
Dee Evans, Richard Godin, Lucy Quinton, Jon Phipps, Chris Tuck, Tony Casement, Rachel Tarkenter, Dave Tarkenter, Pasco Kevlin, Amanda Jones.

ONE

(*Music. He is revealed behind polythene*)

(*ON MIC*) Ladies and gentlemen, welcome. It's truly a pleasure to witness your pleasurable company, in the company of strangers, because for now that is all we are. What then of friendship? Impending? Strangers are far from being friends you haven't met yet. Welcome then again to your everything and anything. Anything your broken hearts desire. For I am your dream-maker, the infiltrator of your darkness, your foetid fantasies and debauchery depravities, your loves, your nightmares. You are made of your experiences and I can cause them, make them and break them. I am your wretch.

I am the man with a laptop full of dirty pictures, who'd cum on your face for a fiver and fuck you in your sleep for less; who'd drop you Rohypnol just to play with you; who'd push you as the train approaches; who'd prey on your weakness and call you anonymously in the dead of night; who'd wink at you and then spit at you; who'd break into your house but steal nothing, empty your bank and then try and help you find out who did it. I'd move the things you put in their place, rub out what you'd written, change the locks and...and you would never know it was me. Because no one truly knows anything, or anyone.

Your expectation alarms me. Somewhere, sometime, some place, some people are waiting for something to happen. To alleviate, I shall begin.

(*Music bangs up. He hacks at the polythene with a knife, revealing himself and the space. He appears lost. He starts to speak, the façade dropped*)

I'm sorry... I... I can't do this... Do you dream? ...can you turn the music off?

(*Music cuts. Light continues to move and then slowly restores to something very general*)

Sorry... I just... sometimes it... Look, I know I'm not doing what I'm supposed to but truly... no, truthfully, I don't care. There, that's rebellion for you. Right from the off. Rebellion and indifference. Lethal combination.

(*He returns mic to stand*)

Do you dream? Real dreams. Not half-thoughts that reappear as *lies*. I'm talking about a real dream, a *truth* that stretches way beyond your acknowledged reality to a point in the extreme distance where you're finally witness to being alive. (*Pause*) I'm not your wretch. You're mine, no, we are each other's, we change each other's thoughts and actions with words and silences, with looks, with manipulation. We are *sent* to the places we don't want to go. Didn't. Didn't want to go. It's past. Past. (*Pause*)

There. I've admitted it. See, I used to think it was me. That my wretch *made* me. (*Pause*) Looking back... bad luck but, again, care? These images...what are they? Memories?... they recreate themselves over and over and I'm sure they're always different. Is that determined by mood? They don't... no, they *won't* disappear. Sometimes good. Sometimes bad. Sometimes... indifferent. There's that word again. Indifference. Never had it so good.

TWO

(*In his space. A derelict room with a sink, a table, a chair, walls and floor plastered with cuttings. There is one window*)

Now. This now is not the same as then. Now is cold. The thermostat? No control. No panic, though. The God pan invades with *his* version of emptiness, but I don't need it. Emptiness is openness and I am awake with my awakened heart. (*Door Knocks*) If you consistently live in the past how can you be in the now? You can't be in two places at once. (*Phone rings*) I will answer the door and I will pick up if I'm in *and* I choose to do so. I am allowed the choice. (*Beat*) I am redeeming myself from the banal, the detrimental, the confusing – No, I am in the *now*. Absolutely in the now - The past – Full stop – The future – Dot, dot, dot – Dot, the music's making my ears bleed. – What is that? It's just for now. The present. The past. Is past. – And there's the music – Am I still bleeding, Dot? Dot? – Gone. She's gone – Again gone. (*Beat*) I used to be that. Gone. I don't need to now. I used to leave the room, go wherever the world took me and do all the things my wretch made me. *Open...* to anything and anyone. Sometimes it would last for weeks. I'd come round in other beds, in other streets, in other countries. No one spoke my language so no one understood. For a time though, it was a wonderful way of living.

THREE

(A Journey. He stands behind the window as if on a bus, looking out. Projection shows his perspective. He holds a blue plastic bag. Sound of traffic)

It's raining. It runs down the glass and the images become unclear. They distort and metamorphose. We are wobbling, vibrations gurgling, squashed against bad colour combinations – or is that art? Immaterial, or so I'd like to think if I could, time is passing and something's impending. This route to morning to midnight to twilight to my light... it drains me. We surface over a brink in a run down a hill before turning left into somewhere... It all passes. I can touch it but the glass is in the way.

(Birds and Music)

Somewhere a man looks through glass down the platform at a girl. I thought it was a bus? No, it's a train running late with its trainers on. The man smiles to himself. It's good to be alive. He cracks open a can of friendship.

(He moves against the wall, as if on the platform. He takes a can of beer, opens it and swigs)

He looks at his watch. It is 8.09am.

(A watch becomes a heart that breaks)

Somewhere a girl's words barely touch a man's heart, so full of hope, but it breaks, irreparably. She doesn't know how it happened.

(*The broken pieces become the time*)

He looks at his watch. It is 8.10am.

A girl stands waiting, beautifully, legs long and wonderfully tanned. Had she been on holiday with the man with the broken heart or had she broken it and then gone on holiday? Her breasts stand out beneath her blouse, large for her frame, but perfect. She is perfect. Full of hopes and dreams her eyes blink into the light and sparkle with rainbows.

(*He drinks*) That girl would love to be understood.

(*SQ: Glass smashes. White noise and fuzz. Something happens. Time jump. In the darkness we hear chaos. Lights come up to reveal him backing away*)

Somewhere a girl is crying and she hides her eyes from a man who knows not what to do. Nor what he has done. What frail days we live in.

(*Behind the window, he is on the street. Sound of traffic. Projection shows his perspective*)

There's a black and white cat peering from a box, late for the vet. It asks for the time but I have to apologise. *Resident Permit Holders Only.* Well, *she* hasn't got one and she's standing nowhere in particular. This rain is such an inconvenience. A man walks slowly along in the middle of the road with a blue plastic bag. The rain, no umbrella. His list of achievements for the day remains unblemished. Perhaps he should resign himself to concentrating harder, to a *see me after class* and head home. I didn't make it though.

FOUR

(In his space, he sits cross-legged, zen-like)

Metamorphoses. Of bodies changed to other forms I tell; you gods who have yourselves wrought every change, inspire my enterprise and lead my lay in one continuous song. The transition from before was difficult, was overrun with difficulty. The past? False beauty, vanity, ego. The quest to be saved, for something to save us all. I thought I knew. Now? Truth. True beauty, true love. Now is the present and I laugh, well, smile, at least inside, at then. It was very funny.

Somewhere a man woke up, I think it was me, and found a small table, a table that was certainly familiar, but he awoke quite calmly, as normal, to find one of the legs of the table imbedded deep into his torso. Now, it was in at an angle and yet all its contents were still in place. Had they been stuck there? Was it magic? An illusion? How did they retain their position on the flat surface when the table was clearly in at an angle? He was puzzled. He checked he was awake. *Am I awake?* he asked. *Yes*, he said. So he was awake. The man had awoken, quite calmly, as normal, to find a small, familiar table in at an angle... and with one of the legs imbedded deep into his torso. *(Beat)* It was like a horror classic. He laughed out loud. It was terribly funny.

(He looks to the pub area)

Once. Once I drowned. Actually drowned. I don't know where I went. I don't think I'd know the difference. Think? No. Would not. Did not.

FIVE

(*Pub noise. He sits at a dirty pub table, with a pint. He drinks and places the glass down*)

There was a circle... on a table, familiar but different. The circle remained from the base of a glass, *my* glass which was attached to my lip. It was a raised circle and I could see the surface of the table submerged inside it... but so too was I... It looked strange, normal, as if through glass, though changed or morphed by the curve of the sides of the circle, by the liquid and I could see my now unattached glass in shards some distance away, but I was unsure if it was the floor or the ceiling. I could see it all though. I could touch it but the glass was in the way.

(*He looks at the rest of the pub. There is a mic and a stage area*)

Or was that the faces? What are you waiting for? (*Beat*) Oh, its Pub Quiz and Karaoke Monday. Big Prizes? Yeh, well your chalk Q is wonky. On your board, the letter Q is wonky. I could do a better Q than that. I could. I do a great Z. Is it Monday? I have no idea how long the day has been. This is not why we are here.

(*Transforms to Karaoke Bar. Cheesy music and projection shows Karaoke slides*)

And which song written by Burt Bacharach became a 1970 *gold* single, selling over 1.8 million copies, listen carefully, but was not sung by him? (*Pause*) That's a tricky one. (*Pause*) A woman claims it was her song... the circle looms...

(*He sings 'Close To You' as the woman on mic, during which she refers to his empty chair, flirting, slowly approaching him*)

I can't hear the words. I have no control... Christ, she's heavy. She grapples at my zip and thrusts her tongue between my teeth. I didn't mean to bite her. (*Beat*) Oi! What did I win? A heated duvet? Oh, well, it is cold. A set of glasses? Fantastic, mine's about to break.

I have no glasses. Therefore I cannot see. I drink straight from the can, when I can't. It induces an urgency. No, darlin', you go on top, I prefer it. It's quicker. That was a rare lie.

(*Music. He reveals a rope which he ties around his wrists and throat and then the same knife. It should represent a kinky, dangerous sex act. He then reveals a plastic bag*)

Asphyxiation can really heighten the experience; it's the deprivation of oxygen to the brain right before one of you cums so you get this incredible sensation just before you pass out. But, the timing has to be impeccable and you really need to be with someone who understands.

(Music. He pulls the bag tight over his face. Slowly he panics, tries to get the bag off, struggles, slowly finding stillness. Dead. He rips the bag off and moves away, referring back to the empty chair)

Her face was distorted, like a baby with a full head of hair. Her face slid off and lodged itself in her cleavage. She was motionless. Well it's so cold, she might have frozen. So many pieces though. *(Beat)* But it wasn't me, you see. I came as she went...went as she came. *(Beat)* The bricks should have done it. She shouldn't have floated. *(Beat)* Well, she was from somewhere else so she couldn't understand. *(Pause)* Was it all you expected, this city of dreams?

SIX

(He looks at photos of a girl. Then at the mirror above the sink)

That's not what happened. / It is. / That is not what happened. / How can you say that? / You're a liar. You didn't do that. You'd have liked to, but you didn't. / Sorry? / A liar. (*Door Knocks. Pause*) Who the fuck are you anyway? (*Pause*) I dunno'. I lost myself in the city somewhere. I looked back and it hurt, so I ran away laughing. (*Door Knocks*) Forever the comedian. No, you were never a comedian. Not a good one. You were the joke. The jokes weren't jokes and they weren't funny. You have to be funny to be a comedian. (*Phone rings*) Yeh, well, whatever. I'm indifferent, its forgotten. It's past.

Fuck, it's freezing and I have no control over the thermostat. Did I win that duvet? The blinds are closed. I don't want the world to see me, nor I to see the world. The glass is in the way but on the ground floor I have no control; the threat of visitors at the door, the phones ring, but there is no conclusion... the pointlessness of these beckoning responses alarms me when I have neither the energy nor the inclination because I still question. The words fall and provoke the images that cause injury, I keep the wound open and feed it until another appears. It's a minor diversion... And yet... no control.

I see myself in front of an audience. My body is full of wounds.

(He moves to the mic and sings Cold 'Bleed'. During which he removes his hoodie to reveal a body covered in cuts, scars, bruises, burns and tattoos)

SEVEN

(Night-time. He stands in moonlight looking out the window. He holds a glass of water)

At night, in the gaze of moonlight flickers, images flit before my eyes, replayed time and time again. The all-consuming light hits the glass, spreads over me and as the city sleeps, I can live out my fantasies. Night into day and back again to the midnight all day, with or without lovers, my pillow my lover, the moon my mother. But it was... *is* never enough. Such pretence. When I crave truth. *(Read from arm)* Echolalia persists but there are no words. *(Beat)* My story book skin. Telling the stories that I can't or that I've forgotten. There was always something, to take away that insatiable need. When I was little I'd cut the skin from my fingers with nail clippers, put peroxide in cuts, I needed to retch so I'd stick things down my throat just to try and get it all out. I liked raw wire on my skin because you can really feel the scratch and the pull. *(Beat)* But it changed... long, complex sessions with big, wide cuts that you could see into, where your body is so shocked by what you've done to it, it takes minutes before it bleeds. It was the control. *(Beat)* See, pain is negation. Against. It's recognised as *not a part of me.* But once the obvious verbal expressions aren't enough pain destroys language and ultimately, self.

(He crosses to sink and washes up a glass)

Then *it* took control; having to succumb as and when, duller blades that hurt more, razor blades that bleed more, burning sessions, the combination of pain, need and thought, ink meeting blood, temporarily delegating control just to get some back. But it was never enough.

(*Holding a glass*)

The glass ceiling. I can touch it but...

(*He starts to rub at the glass, hands unseen*)

Somewhere, a glass is covered in suds, soap suds and suds of soap, washing fairy-up liquid bubbles... and there's hands in there too, holding it, trying to clean, trying to get rid of these stains. But as much as the hands rubbed and scrubbed with suds of soap and soap suds, it remained stained, it wouldn't go away and the fairy-up obscured the view, the clarity of the image... and it changed... there was nothing there... but the glass was broken... and there was blood.

(*He reveals his hand, cut, covered in blood. He stares at it and then, turning away, frantically undoes his trousers and starts to masturbate. He removes his belt, puts it round his throat and continues. Blackout*)

EIGHT

(*In the pub. 'Close To you' plays gently*)

I think I'm still dreaming. Has that woman gone? I can still hear her song in the cables somewhere. (*To the pub*) Turn the music down. I can't hear myself think... You could die in here today and no one would notice. If that man were to slump one way or the other you could literally push him back up again and wedge him against the edge of the window. (*Beat*) When you perceive what you believe to be a party and you wish so very much that you'd been invited, think again. The silhouettes of all the party people enjoying themselves at the window... they could all be dead and wedged. (*Beat*) My mind is giggling. It plays tricks but I can't work out how they're done. (*Beat*) No, it's the children. Where are they? And are they loved? (*Beat*) The familiar glass with familiar distortions. Unbroken. I can see. (*He looks across to rest of pub*) Carefully defined calves, tanned... briefcase, mobile... there's money there, status... she's not happy though... a life running on facades... oh, she's nervous, she's not been here before... oh, she's looking for someone...

The room hits pause and through the imposing mist she approaches me, smiling. Full of hopes and dreams, her eyes blink into the light and sparkle with rainbows. She was looking for me.

(*Stands. A new energy. Direct to audience*)

When eyes meet for the first time a number of things can happen. These things have the potential to be life-changing *or* completely banal. Things like this don't happen in every moment.

Things like this *can* be in the flip of a coin, can happen when the music's too loud or there's too many people getting in the way, be missed and slip away like a dream you can't remember, be taken for granted and slipped into the wallet with the credit cards and photo...

Or...things like this can be cherished and adored, treated gently with clarity and time, with affection, like a kitten or a baby with its first toy... Like a memory you want to hang on to but if you force it it changes. Like hands that make electricity when finger-tips touch and it withdraws all the power.

(*A sense of this slowly happening, things slowing down, power dropping, sounds...*)

The radio falls silent in the middle of a favourite song. The TV goes black as the winner is being announced. The computer crashes before the work is saved. The hairdryer is met with curses when running late. The lights go out.

(*Lights are out. A single light sparks up. The light slowly builds to something incredible, a laser across the space*)

Unaware, somewhere, there is a current across a room. Visible only to two pairs of eyes. So awake, so aware that the world stops turning, mouths stop moving, hearts stop beating, blood stops pumping... but for two pairs of eyes whose mouths say everything and nothing at exactly the same time without even knowing the words, whose hearts beat so fiercely and whose blood pumps like there's no tomorrow. There is only the tomorrow that you want, crave, desire, dream of, and you don't even have to choose because it is yours already and will just be... be in the moment...

...when two pairs of eyes meet for the very first time and a number of things can happen.

(*It crashes. The light falls away. Glass smash. He is back in the pub, clutching his glass*)

But the music *was* too loud. There *were* too many people getting in the way. The kitten ran off and the baby dropped it's toy. The coin landed the wrong way up and the moment *was* condemned to the wallet with the emotional receipts, the credit cards... and the photo of the children... that were never to come. Were they loved? It might have been me but it wasn't enough. Isn't enough. Every time.

NINE

(*In his room*)

The Bible says 'Love keeps no record of wrongs'. But it does. Meticulously. It could do you a lovely pie-chart or powerpoint presentation with no notice whatsoever. It smugly saves them up to hand them out as emotional vouchers to cash in as ammunition.

(*He looks at a photo of a girl*)

I wanted you to love me. But in knowing you only love what you can't have, I couldn't let you know. And through playing games and being dishonest, just to keep you interested... I hated myself... I lost myself... I didn't care... And *then* you loved me.

Love is like a spider's web, it can be pulled down in a glimpse. See, we bend. The neck succumbs to the weight of the head aloft and we bend like a reed in the wind. Oh, we cling on, persuading ourselves that there's a fighting chance as love pokes at us. When is the line drawn? Everyone has their limits. But maybe some are expected to keep swallowing the bad taste of pride and stepping over the line, time and time again. Every time.

(*SQ: Britney Spears – Everytime*)

So, they try to talk, with the inevitable fear of it becoming war and reaching its violent volatile end… and inside, amidst the anger there is the thought: 'This is the one I wanted, for so long. And here we are, together. And realise, at this moment there is nowhere else I would rather be in the whole world and I am utterly, utterly engulfed by a true, true love.'

But I am not asleep and I am not awake as you lie so very far away and I can't reach. The space between two people has never been bigger. I feel sick, paranoid, beaten up, down and inside out… out of a love I am in.

There are no rocks, there's nothing solid to rest upon, so we bend with the reeds, hence exhaustion. There is nothing to say because any word that is retched up is ripped down and it doesn't even land, hence silence.

I miss you more when I see what you have become. And more again when I see what I have become to you. There the tragedy lies. In remembering what I was to you before… before the outside infected you inside… when we are so different… I miss the unspoilt me. Metamorphoses is such a beautiful thing and yet these defence systems are nasty vile inventions full of defects. And understanding only makes it all the harder when you can't get it back, that it, whatever it is… was… its past… And there is no going back because we've forgotten the way there. It is lost somewhere, in the city.

No, one cannot keep returning to the same dirty places. Because as we fight to preserve ourselves, no amount of dirt will make things better.

(*He takes mic and screams out Yashin's version of 'Everytime'. As he replaces mic...*)

That's better.

TEN

(In his space)

No, we are clean and we are each our own friends. Self-sufficient criminals to ourselves. And loneliness is merely pain peering into mirrors of self-pity hoping to see someone to blame it on.

No, the best thing – now – is that I am here – with me – most of the – all of the time. (*Beat*) But no regrets. No looking back... or else the gift might fail. Orpheus and I become one in the same and clasp naught but the yielding air.

Sometimes I think it's the end. There's a scream I can't quite hear. Like a Mandrake torn from the earth that can stop the pain and bring on the deepest sleep. But not now. The unoccupied mind has more time to dwell on the lack of will... to smile, to watch, to listen, to live with or without, to eat, to drink, to try... to even believe anything I have ever thought or written, when I am so hateful and such a liar. It is then that pain quells pain.

Once. Once I drowned. Or was that twice? No, it was an overdose but not meant. A lethal combination, not indifferent.

Once. A man. A boy. Oh, we shared something despicable. In a car park I think. Through the cracks of fog. No, through the fog of crack... it was a mutual ejaculation... but I came as he went... Anyway, he told me that depression is actually a positive thing because its population control. If you are dissatisfied be pro-active.

If you attempt suicide the police will come and take you to jail. Why is it only a crime if you fail? Plus, it is a funeral of choice, so why aren't people more creative? Make it a social gathering. Get the twiglets out.

You could get someone you blame to trigger a noose that hangs you when they open the garage door, so that you're still there twitching when they find you and realise what they've done. It's just a thought. (*Beat*) I have a few more.

(*He takes a piece of paper and it falls open to reveal a vast list of ideas and drawings from which he reads*)

Can we dim the lights, please, thanks.

(*Lights dim as he moves to back wall. Slide sequence*)

Cyanide. Difficult to get hold of but it does get results. It basically paralyses the respiratory centre in the brain. Five hundred milligram's into acid, inhale the fumes, twenty seconds and you're a winner.

Pills – Yeh, a lot of drugs do require prescription but its best to stay away from medical help until you're actually dead. If you take enough iron supplements though, they literally eat a hole in your stomach.

Nitrous Oxide. Well, it would at least mean you go out laughing. (*He laughs*) You could ask your dentist.

Electrocution. Yeh, now I've said this before: Commit, okay. Don't faff about at home, get yourself down to some high tension lines, stand in bare feet on waterlogged ground, maybe with a thick copper cable running into the nearest river and make sure the current travels right through your heart and your head.

Burning. Mix the petrol with an explosive. That is one you don't want to be unsuccessful at. Disfigured for life.

Crushing in a car press. Heatstroke.

I like this one...

Diving. Rising thirty metres without exhaling will usually result in a collapsed lung and death from drowning in your own blood. But... if you can go down further until the oxygen pressure reaches a toxic level *and* you mix carbon monoxide in your tank you can literally go to sleep under water. I think that's beautiful.

(*He moves to the table and reveals a box and during the following meticulously prepares a syringe of smack*)

We each have an emotional and physical pain sensitivity threshold, a censor if you like. But we also have these receptors or locks in the brain. Now, if there were something to unlock them it would be possible to find well-being, elation and, ultimately, less pain. Life would become more significant, divinely beautiful... and earth... well, earth would become paradise.

(*He stands, opens his trousers and injects himself into his groin*)

Diamorphine hydrocholoride, montega, golden brown, black tar, juice, jude, junk, dope, diesel, blow, boy, lady H, ...Goddess of Night, God of Death, of Sleep and of Dreams....

(*He has nodded off, semi-collapsed, shaking... Blackout*)

ELEVEN

(He stands and quotes from news clippings from the wall and blu-tak's others around the space)

'Mother killed 12 year old son with bleach'

'Better to be a lone parent than to row'

'How siblings can shape a child's behaviour'

Where are the children? And are they loved, really loved? Because I can hear crying. *(Beat)* Opium mixed with flies' excrement worked into a paste and taken for four days. That'll stop the crying. That was the Egyptians, not me. *(Beat)* A woman would suffocate her own children, rush them to hospital, dead and then blame staff for not resuscitating them. *(Beat)* A nurse working with terminally ill children would inject them with a heart medication so that he could bring them back from the brink of death.

(He takes a cardboard box from under the sink and places it on the table)

Somewhere a boy and his sister were left with their grandparents. They started having sex at an early age. With each other. *(Beat)* Anyway, their granddad died and the boy believed that his Grandma had killed him. Sometime after, the boy was discovered in a wooden box, kept there by his grandma, because she feared he was damaged.

Is that nature? Or nurture? To split a person in two, to rip apart what is *me* and what is *my body*... making the body *present* and the voice *absent* by destroying them both. That is the essence of torture.

(*He applies make-up*)

There is a basic need to bring meaning to our existence, to define ourselves, which tends to limit freedom rather than help. It helps us to avoid things that might frighten us. And yet, self-knowledge is vital. Choices should not be made out of fear or selfishness. And desires are often influenced by unconscious motives, welling up from our bones. And we can choose how we respond, with a need to understand and not find ways to escape. How can you deny what you feel? Repression has been proved to lead to depression and anxiety, it's been proved.

(*He stands up and pulls a dress from the box. He puts it on*)

So, to resist or to indulge? Existence over essence. Nothing is more important than our reality. We alone must decide what is good and bad for us. We alone.

(*He takes a pair of high heel shoes from the box and sits to put them on*)

Before will there is a wish, to attain something. The will seeks to make the wish a reality. By taking tiny steps what we think we can become, the fantasy, becomes reality. And we... we are liberated. We are transformed.

TWELVE

(*Cabaret club. The sound of an audience. He moves to mic and sings 'Beautiful'. Projection shows his music video, documentary style. The audience erupts*)

(*On mic*) I am not homosexual, nor do I wish to change into a woman. I, mainly, like being a man. I don't feel trapped in a man's body. I have no dysphoria, sometimes a little eu-phoria. (*Pause*) Like I said and I say, transformation is a beautiful thing. I was a star. The media circus rolled in to town and all my dreams came true. I was a fantasy at last.

THIRTEEN

(*Glass smashes. Restores to pub. He apologetically moves to the pub table*)

But it changed. It got cold. My downfall... my downfall was... full of difficulty. Dreams became nightmares and the circus moved on. (*Beat*) We are always driven forward by the mystery and the promise of what lies on the other side. But the illusion is always destroyed when you get what you want. (*Beat*) Some men want to go further than just dressing-up or going out. Some men want sex with a woman... *as* a woman. Some women find this... alarming. And no man should ever force a woman if she falls into this category. (*Pause*) But no regrets. No looking back. Eurydice and I become one in the same, falling, with no complaint, for what complaint had she, save that she was loved? (*Beat*) Nature or nurture. Children are innocent and free and the longer they can stay that way the more likely they are to experiment with wonder. Because either way, the shame and guilt *will* come later.

Oh, turn the music down, I can hear the voices murmuring... / Am I right? Yes, I'm right / And look at my enemies / Don't talk anymore. Are they talking about me? / Oh and isn't it all so very strange! You know nothing. You think you've lived? In my country... ah, you won't understand. You think you've suffered? You have no idea. Do you even understand the English language? Oh, turn the fucking music down... Oh, now you're going?

Where do you live? Nearby? How are you getting there? /
Yeh, see, I know you look at me, you look at me in your
head ...in your head... you're saying ...you're saying
...And you're right...

FOURTEEN

(*He sits barefoot on his table. Brightly*)

There is so much crashing about on false hope or pretence, of *events* that try so very hard to validate a *pan* emptiness. Got to do this, got to go that, perish the thought, got to get a life. Now I am doing this. Can everyone see what I'm doing? I'll do this so that later I can tell them all that I have done it. Oh, but I've already told them. What will they think of me? (*Beat*)

There's no point worrying about what others are thinking of you because they're too busy worrying about what others are thinking of them – and all the things you think they're thinking are the things you think worst of yourself – worry about that or you just might convince them to think the things you think they're thinking.

Its okay, you're a good person. You do belong. And listen, I don't judge, I empathise. Who am I to expose, to initiate immense loneliness and vulnerability? Who am I to unsheathe the chasm of a life so empty and so relentlessly pointless? Who am I? (*Beat*) They never knew it was me. (*Beat*) So many secrets. In places and people, times and towns, the words and the visions consumed into the past but always just a bit too close to the present. It's amazing what one is capable of, the thoughts that come and go, those that are followed through. The extremes of humanity, stretched normality... fascinating and endless.

(*Beat*) Revenge? Sweet? Not really. Sour. And really difficult to plan. But not sweet. (*Beat*) Now I am beyond my enemies and I am grateful to them for allowing me to realise the person I want to be and to practice that. Patience. Tolerance. Compassion. Passion…

Without guilt we lose our humanity. If there is too much, well, there's no redemption.

FIFTEEN

(*The present. He is revealed curled up on the floor in a blanket. Physically much more frail. He retches. Chews on a rotten apple core*)

In exile, a fugitive motel... oh, if I could be metamorphosed into thy shape... The cast of thousands are sending out kisses in imaginary bottles, the wants and wishes of a nation lost in translation... with no one to interpret... there's nothing to say if no one understands. And in the implementation of silence, the words stop. Without one there is no other. And without the other there is nothing. Ditto light. Darkness. Nothing. And nothing... nothing is what? Without the look in the eye there is nothing.

(*At the mirror*)

Looking at a reflection, there is decay. This body, this gift with all its short-lived attempts at improvement, it doesn't even come close. (*Beat*) What if the outside is viewed from in? I can touch it but the glass is in the way. (*Beat*) I wish I could forget all that I know. The fragments still hurt. And I... I don't want to look anymore.

Can you hear me? I have a feeling my words are bouncing off the walls. (*Beat*) Is this a test?

Inside I'm shining. I dance like a madman possessed. Outside I have no need to even nod in time. (*Beat*) Did I pass? (*The sound of footsteps*) Footsteps. A woman's. Will they reach me and stop or will they pass? I feel nervous, like I've done something wrong. (*Pause*) They pass. (*Pause. He looks at the photo of the girl*) Once you reached unbelievable and all-encompassing places in me and replaced the rot with angel dust. But the window wasn't closed properly and the wind just blew it away.

It's all gone long before it's started and I already know the consequences. I feel privileged for having taken part. But there is no belonging. And no surprises.

(*Some of these can be quotes that he has stuck up or written around the space*)

Redemption exists within your dreams, through the fog of sleep, the stories with no end. When loneliness and fear are truly and wholly embraced, knowledge and experience can blossom and perception becomes a state of mind.

Embrace yourself for that is all there is. In craving you won't succeed. Be now and there can be fewer disappointments, less loss and minimal damage. True magic is the magic of reality and becoming one with the elements, mixing your soul with the air, the emptiness. The hidden spring of your soul must needs rise and run murmuring to the sea.

(*He climbs onto the table, feeling it*)

When I have stopped responding, I have no words and no response. To anything. If you have purged everything and everyone, then there's just you. Then surely you are free to do the greater good. Surely. If there's nothing. If there's no one.

I see myself in a ground-floor room full of cold. And when I have no control, with my better part I shall soar above the stars, imperishable.

(*He starts to cry and curls up. Then senses something. He appears to see something above him and is physically drawn towards it, stretching upwards*)

Somewhere Else

First commissioned and developed by Raindance Film.
An early version was first performed at the Cobden Club,
London in 2004

Directed by Gari Jones
Performed by Gary Shelford & Alice Hutcheson

This version was first performed with *Toilet* as part of a
renegade residency at St Martins Church, Colchester on
30th August 2013

Directed by Gari Jones
Performed by James Corley & Caroline Bartleet
Stage Manager Lucy Quinton
Sound Designer Marcus Christensen

Somewhere Else & Toilet thanks to:
Lakeside Theatre, Churches Conservation Trust, Colchester
Arts Centre, Genine Sumner, Barbara Peirson, Harry
Harris, Slackspace, Will Wright, Amanda, Juniper & Milo
Jones, Mr & Mrs Jones, My Icon, Cram Duplication.

This work is part of Renegade, existing to showcase artists and work in all mediums, to provide opportunity, to collaborate and to create innovative work and events. A new way of thinking. A needs must. A sign of the times. An invitation to be heard. Voices in the dark. Fragments rise like moths from the dust.

@renegade_pariah   facebook.com/fragmentsinthedust

Transitions are seamless. HE has a Polaroid camera. Two separate spaces are established. Hers has three candles.

Scene 1

The Present.

HE and SHE in separate spaces.

HE   I remember. The first time I said it was because I should, or thought I should. That it was what couples do. You said it back and we made love like never before and never since.

Pause

The next time I said it was when I realized you meant more to me than anything else. That I would take my life for you, in whatever way you chose. Over the longest time and in the smallest doses.

Simultaneous awareness. They look for something.

We found an understanding unsurpassed and we were one, completely cocooned inside each other, carrying one in the same throughout every day just so we could leave and find each other in the night. Together forever. We were resigned.

Hands and eyes find each other's.

> After a struggle, as much as I resisted, I
> understood its meaning. Forever erupted. Destiny
> failed. My understanding was far more extreme
> than the revelations of a spoken word.

Hands part. Eye contact held.

Scene 2

The Past. He takes a photo of her, breaking the image. They are laughing.

SHE   You still can't say it can you?

HE   I can.

SHE   Say it then.

HE   Why?

SHE   You can't say it.

HE   Why say it just because you say it?

SHE   Say it because you mean it.

HE   When I mean it. Not because you said it.

SHE   I say it because I mean it.

HE   I suggest you say it only to instigate my saying it.

SHE   And when do you say it?

HE   When I mean it.

SHE   When do you mean it?

HE   When I say it.

SHE   But I don't remember you saying it

HE   I have said it.

SHE   When?

HE   I don't remember.

SHE   And if you said it, you meant it?

Pause

       You meant it?

HE   I don't remember...

She walks away.

       ...anything.

He takes a photo of himself.

       Anything.

Scene 3

Street. Rain. Streetlamp. She watches him, unnoticed.

HE   Alone…

SHE   Together

HE   Alone with the alone. The city brims with tortured souls wishing for an end. They could choose, but tend not to. Days don't start or end. Exist and drift in an attempt to survive. Ignore and pretend. Alone and remembering nothing…

SHE   Except me.

HE   …and no one. Those who pretend to care, the dirty observers are all leaving anyway.

SHE   I'm still here.

HE   I've pushed them all away because it hurts too much and I will only destroy them. Want me, need me, love me when I say, for however long I denote and then leave me alone, exactly when I say. Or when I have nothing to say. More and more I have nothing to say because there's simply too much.

Silence.

SHE   I haven't left.

He looks at her.

Yet.

And I'm not dirty.

They smile.

Have you had enough space?

Pause

Would you like to share mine?

HE   Silence is the most resounding word.

They are together. They move to two chairs.

Scene 4

SHE   And they're so in love.

HE   Who are?

SHE   Damsels. In the past. Desperate to see their lover.

HE   Were you?

SHE   They stick two pins, which have to cross through the wax.

HE   This is candles, not voodoo dolls, yes?

SHE   'It's not this candle alone I stick, but my lovers heart I mean to prick. Whether he be asleep or awake, I'd have him come to me and speak.' I think that's beautiful.

Pause

You can read them as well. Uneven burning means danger. Sparks, be cautious. A bright speck, a letter's coming.

HE   From who?

SHE   And if a flame goes out...

HE   What?

SHE   ...great misfortune.

HE   And has yours?

SHE   Has yours?

Pause

And you can use them to summon. A blue flame
means a spirit. Soot on the wick, a stranger.

Pause

HE   Well I hope there's no soot on your wick.

Scene 5

They separate, but remain aware of the other, of being seen or heard.

HE   Together. Is that the right word?

SHE   Alone. Is that the right word?

HE   I think it probably is. Together

SHE   Alone.

HE   I feel sick. Nothing seems real. Seems? Is real. It's a façade.

SHE   The nightmares ebb and flow and cut to the quick.

HE   Secret cravings. Pushed so deep we don't have to acknowledge. Should we even dare.

SHE   They don't stop the attention. A kiss on the forehead. For a moment, it helps.

HE   But in the nightmares…

SHE   But the wounds remain. Sore and vulnerable.

HE   …death is coming. How long will it take? I might get bored.

Pause

I have a madness in my mind. I maintain a haze in order to simply stay alive. Class A's. Although in reality my bank balance won't allow that indulgence on a regular basis. Annoyance doesn't even come close. Denial by a gloating cash point the last time meant I shot everyone else in the queue and raped a cashier. I didn't get arrested though. I ran away. I've never liked the way police stations look on TV. I no longer have a TV. I believe it manipulates the mind and pressures us to want and need the unnecessary.

SHE   The fantasies are coming alive. Somewhere else, alone. Together alone. With another. Please, angel let me be on your mind. Let me be a part of your dreams. Let me keep you awake at night as you do me. Let me touch you in the fog of sleep that has never begun and be there when we don't wake together. How can I love you when I don't know who you are?

HE   People make me want to cry, but I never do. Couples eating in silence, sadness hidden away. They don't know each other and certainly don't love each other. No collaboration. But they accept. Choose. Even singularly. Do they get ulcers? It doesn't relieve the madness, but I'm glad I need and don't when I should. Glad? Contentment is the drug of fools.

SHE   Why do you fill my mind and make me smile, secretly, when you shouldn't. Why shouldn't? Should and do, endlessly, wishing for something, anything... and nothing...but our simplicity of silence. There's nothing to be said. No need. No words can explain or understand this. Why then am I finding so many? Echolalia persists.

HE   There are no words.

Scene 6

The present. Both alone as first image. She lights three candles with a single match.

HE   If I had a sheet I could count the stains. It might help me remember.

SHE has her eyes closed, sensing.

SHE   Where are you? Whoever you are.

HE   But if I did…

SHE   I can feel you…

HE   …I'd remember lost nights and lost lovers…

SHE   …I know you're there.

HE   …and that I created most of the stains myself. Alone.

SHE   Come to me.

HE   Have you ever got home and wondered where your life went and where you were when it was packing?

She opens her eyes.

SHE   You were somewhere else doing the same.

They are in the same space.

HE   How did you know what I was thinking?

SHE   Does counting help you remember?

HE   What were you thinking about?

SHE   When?

HE   You were smiling.

SHE   I don't believe you want to, really.

Pause

       Nothing.

HE   You have the sharpest smile. It cuts to the quick and keeps the wounds open.

SHE   How did you hear me?

HE   You smile at somewhere else.

SHE   I'm here aren't I?

HE   Smile then.

SHE   At now?

HE   Don't.

SHE   Paranoia.

HE   Stop.

Pause

SHE   I love you.

HE   Manipulated.

SHE   Honest.

HE   Forgiven.

Beat

SHE   Backed down.

HE   Beaten down.

SHE   You wish.

HE   Nothing hurts like your mouth. And yet all I do is wish for it. On me.

SHE   I do. I look after you.

HE   Exactly. When my backs to you.

Pause

        Kiss me

SHE   Do you want me to make you cum?

Beat

HE   Fuck

SHE   Its over, isn't it?

HE   What am I going to do?

SHE   We going to do.

HE   I can't function. I'm fucked.

SHE   I know.

HE   I'll never get it fixed.

Beat

SHE   What?

HE   Its broken.

SHE   What?

HE   My bag. My fucking bag. The strap's just come
        away. The metal sheared right through. I've
        already replaced it once. Its ridiculous, its shoddy
        workmanship, that's what it is. I know carry a lot
        in it, just in case, but even so. Sometimes it's so
        full it won't lock. Close, I mean, I wouldn't lock it,
        I might lose the key and then where would I be?
        With a bag full of stuff that I need with no means
        of accessing it. That's where I'd be.

SHE   You're a broken bag.

Beat

        You have no idea who I am.

HE   Nor you I. What I am.

SHE   Where I go.

HE   Who I see.

SHE   What I do.

HE   What I think.

SHE   No idea.

HE   No idea.

Pause

SHE   Try me.

Beat

      You first.

Beat

HE   I am… a junkie

SHE   I'm… I'm depressed.

HE   I am mad.

SHE   I was mad. Now suicidal.

Beat

      I'm a whore.

HE   I was a whore. Now rapist.

SHE   I was raped.

HE   I was raped.

SHE   Really? By men or women?

HE   And then I abducted.

SHE   I abducted.

HE   And I tortured.

SHE   I partook in torture.

HE   Giving or receiving?

SHE   It's much of a muchness.

HE   It is.

Pause

SHE   And then murder.

HE   Murder? Really?

SHE   Absolutely.

Pause

        It was me, wasn't it? Me who you raped, who you
        intimidated, destroyed, defiled...

HE   Kissed.

68

Beat

SHE   Fucked.

Beat

HE   Loved.

Beat

SHE   Loved.

        It was me.

HE   Each of us. In our own way.

        We did it to ourselves.

        We're one in the same.

SHE   The very same.

HE   Then why over?

SHE   Because we had to tell each other.

        We always spoil the end.

Pause

HE   Fuck

SHE   Are we sure?

HE   Fuck

SHE   Are you sure?

        Are you sure we're making the right decision?

Beat

HE   Yes.

        Sorry.

Pause

SHE   I'm grieving. I feel like someone's died.

HE   Sorry.

SHE   Make it go away.

Pause

HE   So many regrets.

SHE   Yes.

HE   And doubts

Beat

SHE   Doubts?

HE   Sorry.

SHE   Don't apologise.

Pause

HE   Its only for the past. We can't allow ourselves to
        regret or doubt
        Or apologise.
        It's all in the past.

SHE   Yes, the past.

Scene 7

HE is watching SHE dancing.

HE Hi.

SHE Hi. I'm Amy. What did you say your name was?

HE I don't know... I don't know you.

SHE No.

HE I'm an amoeba.

SHE A what?

HE Amoeba.

SHE Amy-ba?!

She laughs.

HE Physical. Mental. And sick. Not my fault, though. My little wretch makes me.

SHE Is that what you call yours?

HE Now admitted, I can rectify. There is only the once, after all, until some fuck-up fuck's up and discovers truth in immortality. Only I have to

carry these… things around with me, day after
lonely day. No offence meant darlin', obviously.

SHE   None taken.

HE   Death. It's in the air. Stinks of it. I feel sick.
         Nothing against you, obviously but I think I'm
         going to throw up. (*Pause*) Can you smell it?

She stops dancing.

HE   All you can smell is your sex without me.

SHE   You're a cunt.

Scene 8

He is tied to a chair with tape over his mouth.

SHE   Shh. Silence is the most resounding word.

Do you understand? And don't try and understand completely. Don't because you will to such a massive extent that you will no longer function as even a vague resemblance of a human being. Though what is that? The things that I witness make me question us endlessly. How debauched, how destructive can we, as a race, actually be? You know?

He nods.

Don't you dare to even begin to think you can dismiss it. Accept it, deny it or at least retaliate but don't dismiss it. Okay?

He nods.

You're pathetic, of course it's not okay. Nothing's okay, call that a word? Comment only if you absolutely and completely understand the complexities of this moment...that, that moment.

So?

Pause

So?

She rips off the tape and stares at him impatiently.

HE   I...

SHE   Don't you dare do one of those I dot dot dot's. I despise them. Have a bit of self-respect.

Pause

HE   I think you're a cunt too.

Beat

SHE   You're including me as opposed to excluding me.

HE   I am.

SHE   Unlike you.

HE   Not really. You just don't notice.

SHE   You never told me.

HE   We never tell each other.

Pause

SHE   Have we just..?

HE   Yes.

Pause

SHE   Look at you. What are you up to?

She gets him up.

SHE   Stains on sheets, washing up piling up, not eating, organs rotting and stinking of booze, fags and the sex that's to come...

HE   We're not there yet.

SHE   No, but it's inevitable.

HE   Doesn't have to be. Somewhere else, something else, surely.

SHE   Try.

HE   Because this stinks.

SHE   You stink.

HE   Don't. You stink.

SHE   Why don't you have a shower?

HE   Because you'll leave.

SHE   I'm here aren't I?

HE   You're never here.

Pause

SHE   How do you actually tell someone they stink?

HE   You stink.

SHE   Bit brutal.

HE   Honest though.

SHE   True.

Scene 9

They are together. He photographs her. They are laughing.

SHE   I want...

HE   I want to surround myself with the beautiful and the honest.

SHE   I want to be a seed being blown by the wind on the crest of a wave...

HE   I want to live a lie that I don't know because its not the truth.

SHE   ...deep under the sea with the light flooding down...

HE   I want to squash cockroaches between my teeth.

SHE   ...and crush crabs between my thighs.

Beat

HE   I want to count the stains on the sheets and boast.

SHE   I want to be schizophrenic and addicted and insecure and paranoid and far, far too confident.

HE   I want to be tired and energetic and to explode and implode whilst driving a car and walking everywhere...

SHE   I want to sniff lighter fluid until I don't know who I am and believe I can fly.

HE   I want to tell everyone I'm quite mad and need help as I run along the platform pushing everyone under the tube.

SHE   I want to party forever and run because I've done something wrong, be fucked in the head and absolutely fine and insult a stranger before carving my name into their cheek and tattooing Shakespeare into children's backs.

HE   I want you.

        And redemption.

SHE   You've got it. I want peace.

HE   Of mind?

SHE   I wish that all the destruction and the injustice would just stop.

HE   I want to hold hands with my fellow man, call him a new friend. Wipe my tears from his shoulder.

SHE   But you never cry.

Pause

       I like!

       I like popping unopened coffee but I don't like
       coffee.

HE   I like having a shower and getting so clean my hair
       squeaks but I don't like knowing I've got to get
       out.

SHE   I like telling my secrets to strangers but I don't
       like strangers.

HE   I like waking up next to someone but I don't like
       not knowing who they are.

SHE   I like buying new clothes but I don't like taking
       them back when I discover I don't actually like
       them.

HE   I crave sleep on the clouds in daylight, drowning in
       the endless blue sky. To tell the truth.

SHE   I look at the sky at night, the distant stars and
       crave the space between them and the moon that
       howls until it hurts when there's no choice.

He looks at her.

And yet there always is.

HE   I watch you sleeping, your body moves and your mouth sighs. As discarded shadows of the past unleash your dreams to reveal a thousand stories with no end.

Scene 10

Sun shines. Children playing.

SHE   I want a child. To hold it's tiny hand in mine as I stroke it's head and gaze into it's huge eyes so full of hope for a better life, a touch more understanding and an equation that will grant immortality.

He looks at her, then at the children.

SHE   Hello?

Pause

HE   Hello.

Pause

You're beautiful to me.

SHE   Well thank you.

HE   A beautiful stranger.

Pause

I want to follow you out of view.

SHE   She can see you.

HE   Trap you in a public toilet.

SHE   She can smell it.

HE   Run my fingers down your spine.

SHE   She likes that.

HE   Kiss your neck.

SHE   That too.

HE   And then fuck you...

         ...from behind...

         ...against your will.

SHE   Rape?

HE   That's your word. With my hand over your mouth.

SHE   I'd bite your fingers and draw blood.

HE   Suffocate you.

SHE   With a bag?

HE Transparent. Need to see the face.

SHE Because I'm beautiful.

HE Cum and go at the same time.

SHE I accept.

Pause. They smile.

HE Yesterday I fucked a stranger.

SHE I thought it was me.

HE For hours.

SHE It was me.

ME On the draining-board...

SHE Definitely me.

HE On the floor...

SHE Yep.

HE In the bath...

    On your clothes...

Beat

SHE   Did she piss on you?

HE   I didn't say it was a she.

SHE   Shit on you?

HE   Don't be vulgar. They came when I threw up though.

SHE   Yes, it was me. I threw up. Don't you remember?

HE   I couldn't cum.

SHE   You often can't. It's not your fault.

HE   There is no fault.

Beat

But I played it beautifully and ignored the repetition of 'what's wrong?'

SHE   What's wrong?

Pause

What's wrong?

HE   I... I'm scared.

SHE   Let me make it better.

HE   It's as good as it gets.

Pause

       It's over.

SHE   Over the rainbow. Somewhere, a fountain of
       dreams.

HE   Go and fuck the dog, Dorothy.

SHE   I tried that once. It wasn't the same without the
       cowardly lion.

HE   Don't, please.

SHE   But I can't stand it.

HE   Don't then. End it.

SHE   I don't know how.

HE   Don't be pathetic.

SHE   Don't keep telling me don't.

HE   Don't do it to me then.

SHE   You did it again.

Pause

       Where's this headed?

HE   I wish I knew.

SHE   Stop lying.

HE   Liar.

SHE   I think you know exactly.

HE   Don't.

SHE   Don't don't me.

HE   We just can't face it. The debris.

SHE   How could it happen?

Pause

       Fuck, perish the moment a question might
       actually get answered.

HE   Questions remain unanswered because the answers
        never come. So they remain unanswered questions.

SHE   Do you want this? The prospective plan. Children.
        Love. Shared sleep. Blissful silence. Taking the day
        off so we can spend it in bed and eat biscuits…

Silence. They watch the kids playing.

HE   It's inevitable that you'll move on and engage in
        loads of epic sex. And love it. I can imagine.

SHE   I love it with you.

HE   You don't know any different, do you?

SHE   Don't even go there.

HE   Don't don't me.

Beat

SHE   Anyway, I can imagine.

HE   So…tell me.

SHE   What?

HE   When you fantasize? Masturbate?

SHE   What? When?

HE   Me? All the time.

SHE   Really?

HE   All the time. When you weren't there. Sometimes even when you were. God, its good to talk like this. I did it in all the rooms. Over acceptable magazines brimming with the beautiful people.

SHE   I only ever imagined you.

HE   Sometimes I can't even cum because I've done it too many times already or I simply...can't imagine. Frustration doesn't even come close. They're tastefully photographed, but I make them dirty... imagine their sighs of pleasure as they take me in their mouths, sometimes lying, sometimes kneeling, she lets me thrust into her mouth, she swallows or purposely lets it dribble out, licking at it with her tongue...

She has tears in her eyes. She speaks over him.

SHE   I need you in the night, to support, to nod in the right places, to understand or pretend to, and to get drunk with, to share a cigarette with, to listen to my ambitions, and stroke my back...and be at your beckoned call...hoping you'll be home soon when I don't know where you are and my paranoia creeps in and in the dark, in the silence, in the noise that splinters wood in the smashing of plates in the dripping of the overflowing of emotions hitting the floor and cascading against the walls... I want to be clean.

Scene 11

They are together.

SHE   Scrubbed and clean. And in pyjamas.

HE   And go berserk and never talk and...

SHE   And stand on my head and be a vegetarian meat-eater and

HE   And have no belongings and quote nursery rhymes over a tannoy and...

SHE   And fly to Miami and change my name and make art and...

HE   And smile constantly and need nothing but cottage cheese and...

SHE   And have nowhere to be live and be naked and...

HE   And drink wee and ride bareback and wear dresses and...

SHE   And own a castle and swim in a pool in...

HE   In a volcano and be black...

SHE   And gay and a man...

HE   Who's my sister who's...

SHE   My lover who's my...

HE   My fiancée when...

SHE   I'm old, frail...

HE   Unsuccessful...

SHE   And broke.

Pause

HE   Can you hear it? The silence of a song yet to be
        sung.

They dance.

Scene 12.

SHE   People don't give up. They often reappear through the cracks in the floor, whether you want them to or not, deep scars all over their bodies. But they dress them up in expensive clothes and thicker make-up, still healing from class A wounds, yet maintain a facade of moving on, of change, of renewal.

HE   Hi.

SHE   Hi. Fresh faced, up-and-coming, soon-to-be, sexy smile at virgin dot net.

HE   How's your head?

SHE   My head is completely fantastic and brimming with a thousand new and inventive projects. Social life's blooming. Friends receive negative texts because I simply can't fit them all in. Fashionable clubs, bars til' the early hours. Celebrity chit-chat and mobile numbers exchanged. No sex on first night. That's my rule. Well, unless it's someone really famous and they really want me.

HE   Good. How's your... er...

SHE   My breasts? Oh, my breasts are just perfect now. I've had an enlargement.

HE   The wounds healed?

SHE   On the outside. You can touch them if you like. A
        presenter did last week and he loved them. Then he
        fucked me from behind against my will. But I
        didn't mind really. My legs are perfect too. I've
        had surgery. A pop star adored them. He was
        amazing. After endless lines of coke he was still
        hard for hours. He told me and then he punched
        me. He made me bleed.

HE   Stop it.

SHE   Am I the most perfect creature on earth? Do you
        completely and absolutely adore me? I'm a good
        person, aren't I? I am, aren't I? Just tell me.

Pause

        I just want to make you happy.

Silence. They hold each other.

SHE   Sorry.

HE   No. I'm sorry.

They kiss.

HE   I don't know you.

SHE   Neither do I.

HE   You're a stranger.

SHE   I'm a stranger.

HE   What does she want?

SHE   To be wanted.

Pause

HE   You're mouth.

Pause

SHE   Tastes horrible.

HE   Me?

SHE   And me.

HE   As one?

SHE   No. They don't mix.

She dribbles.

SHE   You.

She spits.

SHE   Me.

HE   Again.

She spits.

SHE   Me.

HE   Where am I?

She looks to the floor.

SHE   There. Don't mix.

HE   Don't or won't?

SHE   Don't.

HE   I'll make them.

He goes to hit her. Can't. Leaves.

Scene 13

They are in their separate spaces.

SHE   It's lonely. At night. I can't sleep. Images won't let
      me.

HE   What's normal? What's madness? The bodily
      fluids don't mix but they've lubricated each other.
      The combined complexities create another. But its
      all in the cables anyway. And we are obsolete.
      This? This is just psychic litter.

SHE   I think of you sat in your chair, writing, watching
      you when you didn't know and smiling.

HE   I think of you looking beautiful in a doorway when
      we first met and i remember exactly what you
      were wearing.

SHE   I think of you decorating the Christmas tree and
      dancing to Nirvana.

HE   I think of you having flu and stroking your head
      and buying you Smash Hits.

      I miss you.

Scene 14

He takes photos as she holds up objects and finally his teddy.

SHE   Do you want nothing?

HE   What for?

SHE   I don't know, fondness? I just can't believe you can discard us so easily.

HE   We are not things.

SHE   Memory?

HE   Memory? What, trying not to cry when you said you needed space and I said I'd try and understand.

SHE   Yes, just after you told me you'd slept with a girl I hated but it didn't mean anything.

HE   And you explaining you'd fucked a stranger when you were away and claimed you were missing me.

SHE   I was missing you.

HE   Before or after he'd shot his load?
Before or after he'd shoved his dirty water up you?

Pause

SHE   Well, you say something then. How many others were there?

HE   I don't remember.

SHE   But you remember her?

HE   Her? Yes, of course. She... she had a figure to die for.

SHE   And I think you did.

Why not the others?

HE   What others?

SHE   So is this you telling me you strayed once out of retaliation, had a snog because you didn't know what you were doing?

HE   Oh no, I knew exactly what I was doing.

SHE   You did?

HE   Yes, exactly. I fucked her until she came.

SHE   That's a first.

HE   It was exact. Until she came.

        And then I fucked her until I came.

SHE   (*Overlapping*) Until you came. Yes, I get it. Well
        done.

HE   She was exquisite.

SHE   I don't want to know.

HE   Tits, legs and arse to die for. And you're right, I
        did.

SHE   After you'd fucked her?

HE   I thought you didn't want to know.

        But she wanted me. Wanted me to stay. She
        begged, literally begged me. Cried and cried.

        It was shocking.

        Makes you realize, don't judge by appearances.

Pause

She holds up a teddy

SHE   Well, you can't throw him away, you've had him
        since you were a baby.

HE   Exactly. Get rid of it.

SHE   I'll have him then.

HE   What will you do with it?

SHE   Sleep with him.

HE   It'll only get shoved out when you start fucking
        your new fuck.

Pause

        I'll take him.

SHE   Why now?

HE   The beds half-empty.

SHE   Without me.

HE   Of course without you.

SHE   It's a single.

HE   There's room for him. Still sleep alone.

SHE   Me too now.

HE   Where?

SHE   I have no idea. You've made me homeless. And
      you owe me an awful lot of money.

HE   For what?

SHE   For the deposit and the rent in advance and for
      dinner last week and a third of the duvet cover and
      the fairy lights and sixty three pints of cheap lager
      and thirteen copies of smash hits and a packet of
      condoms and an abortion when they broke and the
      train fairs and tissues when you made me cry and i
      wanted to see my mum and the present for your
      brother and the veggie burgers when you didn't tell
      me you'd started eating meat and for supporting
      you when you decided to be a writer and the pain
      and the laughter and the damage and the constant
      fucking excesses you continue to fill your life with
      in order to try and cope with a reality that disturbs
      you so extremely and makes you so selfish and so
      revolting that I can honestly say I hate you.

HE   If I have nothing, then I want for nothing.

      Please leave me alone.

Scene 15

SHE   Have you still got him?

HE   No.

Pause

      Can you hear it?

SHE   What are the words? Oh yes, there are none.

HE   I cannot be with you.

SHE   You cannot be with *me*.

HE   *Be* with you.

SHE   Be *with* me.

HE   I was never with you.

SHE   You were never with me.

HE   There were too many strangers getting in the way. Once you've seen the world for what it is... together becomes an impossibility. Normality barely exists. It's all mixed up to create another...

SHE   Love? As opposed to...?

HE   This love.

SHE   That.

Pause

HE   You'll cry. All the time. Be unable to function.

SHE   You'll drink. All the time. Self-destruct.

HE   Then you'll recover, become excessively independent, get fit, buy a house, find a lover and control him.

SHE   You won't eat, you'll chain smoke and live for your art, vomit when you wake before drinking again, contemplate suicide all the time but not do it because you wouldn't be able to hate yourself for not doing it...and you will get sick.

HE   I said I would. In whatever way you chose.

SHE   I never had a choice.

HE   Are we sure?

SHE   Look at us. The final cliché.

HE   Why do you think this is any easier for me?

SHE   Don't assume it's harder for me.

HE   I just want to try and understand.

SHE   I've done nothing but understand. I'm sick of understanding. I can understand nothing else.

HE   We can be there for each other. Whenever, whatever you want.

SHE   But I want you and I can't have you so you're a liar.

HE   We can still be friends.

SHE   More clichés. Friends who support each other and talk about films and lovers.

Beat

I can't even bare to think of you with someone else.

HE   There won't be. Not like we were.

SHE   So you're going to stay single, are you, sleeping your way through the entire female population?

HE   Look, call me whenever you want.

SHE   There's nothing else to say.

HE   Well this can't be it.

SHE   You'll find someone.

HE   So will you. You're beautiful, talented, funny, intelligent. Who wouldn't jump at being with you?

SHE   You.

Pause

        Do you miss me?

HE   Very much.

He takes her photo.

SHE   I still love you.

Pause

        You still can't say it, can you?

She cries.

HE   Go on. Go.

Pause

I'll speak to you soon.

She watches him leave. He gives her photos and camera.

Scene 16

The present. He holds the teddy bear. She lights three candles with a single match.

SHE   I can hear the words.

HE   Redemption.

She smiles.
He cries.

The End

TOILET

Originally commissioned by Menagerie Theatre Company
An audio version is currently online recorded by Frequency
Theatre.

Directed by Nick Barton-Wines
Performed by Gari Jones.
Produced by Bethany Sharp-McLeod

First performed with *Somewhere Else* as part of a renegade
residency at St Martins Church, Colchester on 30th August
2013

Directed and Performed by Gari Jones

Stage Manager	Lucy Quinton
Sound Designer	Marcus Christensen

A man in a tiny cubicle, walls tight to him. He sits on a lavatory, trousers round his ankles. Debris covers his feet and the floor.

A constant soundtrack from 'outside' surrounds him and changes throughout, following his mood, sometimes as if that's the music in the party, other times as a soundscape to his imagination.

Initially, a full-blown party can be heard outside, loud Dubstep music playing, laughter, talk.

Am I at the beginning? Or the end? In the middle. The start of something. No, the middle. On an axis that turns and hits points around its circumference. Is that it? Can I choose?

Still alive?

He checks and feels his body. Relieved.

I sit exactly half way on a road to nowhere. It's not an age thing, this half way; it's a depth of feeling, an overwhelming desire to reassess. I am reassessing.

Enclosed in safety – am I safe? – safe from what? Outside. And outside is what?

Pause. Sound changes.

The waste leaves me and a peace descends. Momentarily.

Pause

My mind is crammed with a web of thought, strings of excitement, hope, fascination are interwoven with a bleak doom of a cloud that plagues me daily. It's been a while, maybe years, since the reality of this, a dead-set chasm such as this took up nesting space. But now, here it is and daily, truly, daily do I struggle with the brave face and cracked smile, energy sapped as my vessel creaks and moans through every step, every gesture as my darling children want to run and climb and chase and hide and laugh and... hence my struggle, to keep on keeping on...

A phone beeps. He takes it from a pocket and looks at it. A text message.

How long have I been here?

Light and sound crash in.

The wall opens. No, not the wall, the *door*. They're doors you fuck, it's a fucking door. The door opens. Excuse me, says the voice and steps over my thighs, my legs. I try to cover my modesty.

Light and sound restore.

I am disturbed by how susceptible some people are. Or is that gullible. To believe and then blame and have to complain at the mass deception. Sale must end tomorrow, tomorrow comes and on it goes. Half price, two for one, great deal, special, special offer. Oh, but the high streets are in crisis. We've been told. A glass of wine will cure cancer. Don't drink wine, it'll make you rot. Don't leave your house, you'll get run over, the roads are lethal, there's too many cars. You'll be bombed, they're everywhere those type. The sky will cave in, it's been damaged. You'll be poisoned by the air, it's polluted... poisoned by the sight of your neighbour... paedophile, murderer, rapist, thief... you can't trust anyone. We read, it says, we believe, it says... fear. So much fear. Because it says.

Unemployment up by 8%, incomes fall by 3.5%, immigrants removed down by 13%, immigration up by 4%, divorces up 4.9%, fake marriages for illegal immigrants up by 54%, arrested child sex offenders up 10%, shoplifting up 20%... The number of journalists imprisoned worldwide... up 20%.

Pause. Light and music change. Time pass. He shifts. The façade drops.

I haven't slept for weeks. This morning I heard something. A door opened somewhere. A sound like plastic crackling. Pebbles. Footsteps on pebbles. Plastic dragging. A boot opened, a car boot. Plastic, breathe, plastic, boot shuts.

The car drove away. It was the sound of my neighbour putting a body in the boot of his car.

Neighbours speculate as to their neighbours comings, goings. Doings. The curtains remain closed so there's little to see. Isn't that always the way?

Beat

I too scrutinize. A body, another body, *another's* body. Search, claw and pull at it as if wanting to find a zip and climb inside. But only when its passive. As soon as it starts *doing*, all interest is lost. As soon as it thinks it becomes fragments of thought. The body is divided. Skin, calves, thighs, eyes, throat... mouth, the voice unknown, the possibilities of a body, equally unknown, but easily imagined. So it is mine. Mine to mine, mine becoming a vessel for another.

Sound changes

The bodies pile up. There's a war. A constant war. Piles of bodies litter the earth, dead and alive, flesh and skin crawling, pressing, pressed together. Contaminated and diseased. The flies are in their element, the maggots surge forward as the vultures start to circle overhead.

These are my neighbours. Leaking stories that drip years of callous and horrific acts of structured abuse and torture, of suffering, of deaths, toll numbers changing like TV channels, like a lottery, and every one a life. Everyone was a life, with a heartbeat, a family, a child perhaps, a child *to* someone perhaps. Every one perhaps. Wars based on lies. These are my neighbours.

A blindfolded man sits in a line of hundreds awaiting his turn. His fate. Isn't that always the way?

Either way, the wrong people hang.

His phone rings. He speaks over it.

See, with one image I manage to annihilate another. Completely. Another time another image compliments. They combine and become one or else contradict and their entirety communicates something other that on their own they cannot. That is something beautiful.

Phone stops ringing. Relief.

Peace sits in an armchair while empathy and compassion are cuddled up on the sofa. They watch arrogance and self-loathing have a face-off, each daring the other to go first.

He smiles. Tries another

Rebellion ran away laughing. But personality couldn't catch him as numbness held on to his hood and complacency tripped him up.

Light and sound flood in

Again the wall, sorry, the *door* opens, the other side. 'Sorry, darling' and high heels tiptoe across in front of me. No chance of a cover up. 'Nice', says the voice. I smile. The wall, door, closes.

Light and sound restore

If I stay long enough will it all go away? Will the burdens be shed like a reptilian paper skin? Or will the crucifixion await my weight regardless with a salivating mob of onlookers wanting justice?

Missed payments. So many. On debts. On credit cards. On loans. On the interest. On the charges. On the mortgage. On the debt collections. On the bailiffs. On the beggars. On the coppers that bounce across a pavement at the feet of my children, left to fend for themselves amongst the scraps of humanity.

I am no different, we are all in debt. The country is in debt. To who, the world? No, the world is in debt. Debt crisis. Recession. There's less than no money and people are dying. 'Economic uncertainty'. House prices plummet. No one's buying. The streets are in chaos, rioters and the desperate see a way and choose it. Why not? Its circumstantial. Greed. In that there is recognition. Wanting and taking. Taking and wanting more.

Phone beeps. A text message. He reads it. He shifts. Music changes.

The love that once resounded so loudly in echoes, is now entirely without resonance.

I took her head in my hands, her face in my hands, between my fingers. And I looked. So hard I looked. And as I removed my hands, it floated. Her face floated.

No, you're wrong, she said. It is still on. Firmly, still on.

I love you, I said, so much it hurts. It was a desperate love cry, a repetitive utterance, like a child, socially irresponsible. It has nowhere to go as a phrase and so is delivered merely for response, when there is none. I wanted my desire satisfied immediately, no, before I'd even said it I wanted response and reciprocation.

But I am so tired of you. I dream of you, have thoughts of doing things to you, with you, that I could never ever articulate. But it has nowhere to *go*, these things have nowhere *to go*. Where can it, does it, go?

Sound changes

I have nowhere to go.

Did he cum inside you?

No.

So he came *on* you?

Yes.

Beat

It'll be alright. I'll make it alright.

Pause

You're right. It will be all-right.

You forgive me?

It will be alright because I've done that a thousand times
with a thousand people. In unimaginable positions and in
the most absurd and wonderful, curious places. So, yes, it
will be alright.

Beat

So many. I fucked an entire country once. Or was that
fucked up? But the curious thing is that I don't remember
any of them. Isn't that always the way?

Beat

Am I lying?

Beat

So many faces that once meant so much, friends, lovers, family, all gone. What happens, what changes, that they just go? Sentiment is for fools. They disperse in a fog for another few years until they're coughed up, begging to be seen once more.

Music and light change. He shifts. Time pass.

How long have I been here? It stinks.

He closes his eyes.

I love the smell of... freshly opened coffee... clean sheets... my wife... *ex*-wife's moisturiser... my baby's head... *a* baby's head...

Pause

There's something in here that's mine. *Was* mine. In its leaving have I discarded it for another to claim? It is semen, blood, urine. It is excrement. It is tears. A veritable cocktail of body. It is there. I like the fact that it is there.

He smiles

I won't flush.

Sound changes

An examination we sit, to answer the possibilities, the possibility of answering, actually answering who we are, actually, are; that pushes, no, *probes* to see what happens, what reactions, behaviour, the nature of the behaviour, its delicacies, simplicities... we, the watchers, the loggers, the watchers and the watched... I don't know what I'm trying to say... I can't formulate the... the...

Beat

Merely, that it is all perceived, all perception. Isn't it? One version of events, one version of speculation, of action, of behaviour. Just one. At any one time.

Beat

Or a combination, at any one time.

Whilst we are free to choose our own course we are not free to violate our nature, our moral nature. That is not authentic. You violate what you believe to be right or wrong, to justify, to reach an end result. It does not need to be an escape to freedom where there is no moral judgement. Or responsibility. Where is the responsibility?

Beat

Exactly.

Our existence is profound, isn't it? Deeply. What we choose to do with our time... it... it matters. No blame. No hiding. No pretence.

Music changes

I am every man. It was me. It was me who was maimed, who was tortured, raped, murdered. It was me who was thoughtful, ambitious, unsuccessful. It was me who dreamed. Me who was ecstatic, liberated, found. It was me who was loved.

In years to come in a note to myself, the words: Conquer your dreams, suppress your insecurities, repress your speculations, ignore your enemies; they will only damage themselves. Remember the best bits, forget the rest. And regret nothing.

The End